1666

REDEMPTION

THROUGH SIN

Robert Sepehr

Printed in the United States of America

First Printing, 2015

ISBN 978-1-943494-01-9

Atlantean Gardens
5334 Lindley Ave #133
Encino, CA 91316

www.AtlanteanGardens.org

Table of Contents

Introduction

Most people have heard of Jesus Christ, considered by Christian followers to be the Messiah who lived over 2000 years ago. But very few people have ever heard of Sabbatai Zevi, who declared himself to be the Messiah in 1666. He amassed a following of over one million believers, half the world's Jewish population during the 17th century, by proclaiming that redemption was available through acts of sin.

Considered a heretic by many of his contemporary Rabbis, nonetheless, his fame extended far and wide. Sabbatai's adherents planned to abolish many of the ritualistic observances, because, according to the Talmud, in the Messianic time there would no longer be holy obligations. Fasting days became days of feasting and rejoicing. Sexual promiscuity, adultery, incest and religious orgies were encouraged and practiced by Sabbateans.

After Sabbati Zevi's death in 1676, his philosophy would be continued, and expanded on, by his Kabbalist successor Jacob Frank. Frankism, a religious movement of the 18th and 19th centuries, centered on the leadership of the Messiah claimant Jacob Frank. He, like Zevi, would perform strange acts that violated traditional religious taboos, such as eating fats that were forbidden by Jewish dietary laws, ritual sacrifice, promoting orgies and sexual immorality.

Jacob Frank would eventually enter into an alliance formed by Adam Weishaupt and Meyer Amshel Rothschild called the Order of the Illuminati. The objectives of this organization was to undermine the world's religions and power structures, in an effort to usher in a utopian era of global communism covertly ruled by their hidden hand: the New World Order. Using secret societies, such as the Freemasons, their agenda has played itself out over the centuries, staying true to the script. Opposition is handled by a near total control of the world's media, academic opinion leaders, politicians and finance. While still considered a conspiracy theory to many, more people are waking up each day to the reality that this is not just a theory, but a true conspiracy.

Chapter 1

In 1666, an exceptionally charismatic Rabbi and Kabbalist by the name of Sabbatai Zevi (1626-1676) declared himself to be the Messiah. Born to an affluent family in Western Anatolia, he was a particularly eccentric mystic who had attained a massive following of over one million devotees during his lifetime, roughly half of the world's Jewish population in the 17th century. (1)

His extraordinary popularity, according to historians such as Professor Gershom Scholem, resulted largely from the publication and availability of what is today called the Lurianic Kabbalah.(1) Named after Rabbi Isaac Luria (1534-1572), this new Kabbalah enjoyed broad dissemination thanks to the invention of the printing press in the previous century. Jews around the world for the first time had access to occult literature about the deeper meaning of their faith and the popularity of Jewish mysticism soared. After a particularly harsh period of persecution in European history, this pro-active Kabbalistic philosophy, through an ancient mystical system, gave Jews a reason to be excited and optimistic.

Part of this system included ways of interpreting the supernatural relationship between events and time; often through letters and numbers.

FIGURE 1

The 'magical' emphasis given to the numerological value of dates contributed greatly to the widely held expectations and hope placed on the coming of a Messiah at the time of Sabbatai Zevi's advent the 18th day (6+6+6), of the 6th month, of the year 1666. (1, 8)

Zevi was extremely charming and exuded an inviting personality, as documented by those who knew him. According to an eyewitness, Rabbi Leib ben Ozer:

> You must believe that this was how it was. I spoke with people who ate and drank and were near him, who were not proponents [of Sabbatai Zevi's] and they told me that there was none like him in stature and in the way his face looked, like that of one of God's angels. And they testified that when he sang Sabbath hymns to God, which he did several times a day, it was not possible to look into his face, for one who looked at it, it was as if he looked into fire. (1)

Sabbatai Zevi was considered very handsome in appearance and also possessed an enchanting singing voice. Rabbi Leib ben Ozer goes on to describe another phenomenon which added to belief in Zevi's messianic claim:

> And this is one of the greatest occurrences, clearly super-natural, that came to pass in those days and a reason for the great belief in Sabbatai Zevi, for it happened in many places, that prophets arose in hundreds and thousands, women and men, boys and girls and even little children; all of them prophesied in the holy tongue [Hebrew] and in the language of the Zohar as well, and none of them knew a letter of Hebrew and all the less so the [idiosyncratic] language of the Zohar. (1)

Many Rabbis of the time publicly attested to having had dreams in which Sabbatai appeared to them, sometimes by the side of their bed, and when they awoke they would profess that he was the Messiah. According to professor Gersham Sholem, a sincere expectation arose in the psyche of many Jews, especially in Europe following the Spanish Inquisition, that Biblical prophecy would be fulfilled via a Jewish homeland. (11)

According to some critical interpretations of his behavior, Sabbatai showed signs of what modern scholars would likely call manic-depressive psychosis. In other words, he publicly displayed at times ecstatic behavior, often followed by bouts of seclusion or possibly depression. He also violated numerous religious laws, from dietary restrictions to committing acts of sexual immorality. (1, 8, 11, 13)

On the other hand, some scholars and modern day followers, or neo-Sabbateans, have argued that his behavior did not point to psychosis, but rather, was simply what one should expect from of a religious mystic, such as a Sufi: meditative chanting, prayer-trance, dancing, etc. According to professor Avraham Elqayam, faculty member of the Jewish Philosophy Department at Bar-Ilan University in Israel, Sabbatai engaged frequently in Bektashi Sufi rituals. This perspective seems reasonable to me, as Sabbatai Zevi's final grave sight in Albania was made into a Sufi shrine, as it remains even today. (5)

In any event, Zevi's unusual, or socially immoral and religiously unacceptable behavior finally got him expelled from Smyrna around 1650, and he wandered for years through Greece, Thrace, Egypt, and Syria. In 1665 his life forever changed upon meeting Nathan of Gaza in Palestine, the Rabbi who persuaded him that he was indeed the Messiah to usher in a new age, and who would become known as one of his greatest proponents and interpreters. Sabbatai Zevi was convinced and formally revealed himself after considerable encouragement from Nathan, making his pronouncement in the year 1666 as to fulfill Messianic prophecy. He soon gained fervent support in the Diaspora (areas outside Palestine settled by Jews) by promising a return to a Jewish homeland, a message that was then well received. (8, 11)

Despite his strong support and popularity among the Jewish people, the leading Rabbis of Jerusalem rejected Sabbatai's claim as Messiah. They basically told him to leave the city, or be excommunicated. Very disappointed, but undeterred, Sabbatai returned to Turkey, where the Sultan of the Ottoman empire had already allowed the Zevi phenomenon to unfold for several years.(1,8,11) The Sultan did not initially oppose Zevi's religious claims, probably because those claims brought in so much money from Jewish tourism, as Jews flocked to Turkey from from all over the world, from England to Persia, Germany to Morocco, Poland to Yemen. (11)

FIGURE 2

Though at first the Sultan did not interfere with Sabbatai's movement, the last straw came, according to one of many rumored accounts, when Sabbatai publicly proclaimed that, in next year, the Temple in Jerusalem would be rebuilt. The Sultan took umbrage. The most commonly accepted version of the story is that the Sultan offered Sabbatai Zevi the choice of either publicly converting to Islam or being beheaded. As the Sultan so delicately put it: "Your head or the turban."(11) The turban was, of course, a symbol for converting to Islam. Sabbatai Zevi, the supposed long awaited Messiah, denounced his Jewish faith on the spot, and chose to wear the turban and keep his head. Zevi publicly became a Muslim and adopted a new name: Aziz Mehmed Effendi ("Power of Muhammad"). The Sultan gave him a reasonable salary as the Sultan's personal doorman, and the cryptic title "Keeper of the Gate". All the while, it seems he continued in his messianic activities, acting with, one must assume, the full knowledge of the Islamic authorities. (8)

Sabbatai may have converted to escape execution, but Nathan and his other loyal followers put a different interpretation on this transition. According to them, Sabbatai's conversion represented the descent into the klippotic realm ("grossest" reality, or "husks" of creation) in order to reclaim the lost 'sparks' of divine light, which is meant to 'repair the world'. These are Kabbalistic concepts which most modern scholars have concluded were all too often used to justify his heretical and socially radical behavior. (1,2,3,8,10,11,13,24,26,30)

Sabbatai's formal conversion to Islam dismayed many of his followers, to say the least, but those who continued to be loyal to the movement took it as a sign to also convert to Islam, while secretly maintaining their Jewish identity and mystical practices. The most famous of these Sabbatean cults, as they were sometimes called, was primarily located in Anatolia (modern Turkey). Detractors called them the Donmeh, which translates to 'religious converts', a derogatory term which they themselves never used.(36)

Nathan's optimistic interpretation of Sabbatai's change of faith did not sit well with most Jews, but it did find a great degree of acceptance in places like Spain and Portugal, among the 'conversos' (converts) and Marranos, two names for western European Jews who were forced to convert to Christianity during the Inquisition.

According to Reb Yakov Leib HaKohain, the current director of Donmeh West, a Californian neo-Sabbatean organization founded in 1972:

◇◇◇

It is commonly held conjecture that Sabbatai Zevi's conversion to Islam was an act of cowardice that betrayed the Jewish people. However, this 'conversion' was not an act of cowardice, but in fact one of the mystical ma'asim zarim (strange actions) that he and Nathan of Gaza believed the Messiah was destined to perform, based on their reading of the Kabbalah. (5)

◇◇◇

Such an unorthodox and controversial explanation suggests that the collapse of Sabbatai Zevi's world-wide movement, and almost of Judaism itself, resulted not so much from what Sabbatai did, as from the inability of the Jewish people to understand and accept it. In other words, it was not Sabbatai Zevi who "betrayed" the Jewish people, but they who misunderstood and, therefore according to Mr. HaKohain's view, abandoned him.(5)

Sabbatai Zevi, like the Sufi mystics, used to loudly exclaim words of ecstasy. Sabbatai was said to have taken part in the Sufi Bektashi rites conducted at Adrianopolis. In many ways the Sunni majority considers the Bektashi Order and Alevis antinomian ("lawless"), so it is interesting that Sabbatai Zevi chose to affiliate with them.(3) In many regards, the Bektashi-Alevi Sufi fall beyond the limits of acceptable Muslim behavior. Many Bektashi-Alevi do not follow the prescribed five daily prayers, preferring instead to offer their prayers privately or at Cem, the religious gathering place of the Alevi. Nor do they adhere to fasting during Ramadan. Many Bektashi-Alevis drink alcohol and do not regard it as sinful, unlike the majority orthodox belief.(4) They also emphasize the equality between men and women, who may practice together in the Cem and in Zikrullah (the gathering for Zikr). For the pilgrimage or Hajj to Mecca, they substitute a pilgrimage to the shrines of Sufi saints, or visits to living Babas or Dedes, their religious elders and leaders.(4)

The notion that Sabbatai held Sufism in high regard, and practiced it's Gnostic techniques, is one that professor Gersham Schalom seems to have failed to notice, or adequately bring to light. The goal of this spiritual conversion, according to many modern Donmeh, was to bring about a sacred reconciliation between two religions, rather than to practice either. The theory is that one accomplished this by internalizing an opposing or "alien" religion into one's own person in order to reconcile inwardly what is outwardly antagonistic, thereby reconciling two seemingly opposite systems and raising up the 'holy sparks' in each to their source. (5, 11)

But what are these 'holy sparks' and where did they come from? Isaac Luria, whose interpretation of the Kabbalah is now most widely used and

FIGURE 3

accepted, explained that God created the world by forming 10 vessels to hold the 'Divine Light'. God intended this original Light to radiate out, fill the world and illuminate everything around us. But as God poured the Light into the vessels, the Divine Light was so powerful that the vessels couldn't contain it. With a huge explosion, the vessels shattered and sparks of this Divine Light became imbedded into the world of matter. (5,11) The material world had trapped these sparks of Divine Light; God's presence was hidden and unable to shine forth. It then became the task for us (presumably the chosen ones) to free these holy sparks. The manner in which people approached and interacted with the material universe could set these sparks free and repair the world. (36)

Another key aspect of Isaac Luria's interpretation, now known as the Lurian Kabbalah, is that it required active participation to set the stage for the arrival of the Messiah. He designed his new Kabbalistic instructions for liberating holy sparks to bring about the conditions that would set the stage, initiate, or directly expedite, the fulfillment of Jewish messianic prophecy.(28) In other words, instead of simply waiting for God to act, the Lurianic perspective expected Jews to play an active role in bringing forth God's kingdom on earth. This new European Kabbalah, unanimously attributed to Luria, was extremely popular at the time and is still the most broadly disseminated and used Kabbalistic system taught.

FIGURE 4

The Kabbalah became a mystical synthesis between pagan teachings which preceded the Torah, and Gnostic elements of Judaism. Many texts pertaining to the Kabbalah, including the Zohar, say that the task is not to destroy evil but to return it to its source. To put it simply, to "include the left within the right," in the Zoharic metaphor, or "to uplift the fallen sparks" in the Lurianic one. (11)

The occult scholar, mystic, Orientalist and renowned author of *The Secret Doctrine*, Madam H.P. Blavatsky commented that:

Mistaken is he who accepts the Kabalistic works of today, Kaballah and the interpretations of the Zohar by the Rabbis, for the genuine kabalistic lore of old! For no more today than in the day of Frederick von Schelling does the Kabalah accessible to Europe and America contain much more than ruins and fragments, much distorted remnants still of that primitive system which is the key to all religious systems. (18)

Madam Blavatsky added that the Chaldean was the oldest, and likely the most authentic version of the Kabbalah:

The Chaldean Kabbalah, moreover, the Book of Numbers, agrees perfectly with the eastern arrangement, and disagrees with the present orthodox Kabbalah in its diagrams. I saw they had changed it in the most wonderful way, the Kabbalah was entirely lost. Now, in the Chaldean Kabbalah, in the Book of Numbers, you have the wisdom of the Hebrew initiates, but you have not got it in this [i.e. the modern, popular, and accepted versions of the Kabbalah]; they have been so interfering with it.. I say there is more flapdoodle than truth. (18)

The rapid spread of the teachings of Rabbi Isaac Luria and his Lurianic Kabbalah resulted in a grafting of the then current theories of the Kabbalist onto the traditional Jewish view of the role and personality of the Messiah. This new philosophic paradigm, in the estimation of many scholars, provided a spiritual justification for proactive Zionism and the events that directly brought about the modern formation of Israel. (8)

Mystical Lurianic speculations about the nature of the redemption, and the 'restored world' (olam ha-tikkun) which follow upon its heels, added new content and dimensions to the popular messianic folk-myth of a conquering national hero, raising it to the level of a supreme cosmic drama.(27) The redemptive process no longer simply worked out Israel's temporal emancipation from the yoke of the Gentiles, but rather it involved a fundamental transformation of the entirety of creation, affecting material and spiritual worlds alike, and would lead to, in the words of Gersham Scholem: "A rectification of the primordial catastrophe of the breaking of the vessels (shevirat ha-kelim), in the course of which the divine worlds would be returned to their original perfection." (1)

This process is called 'tikkun olam', or 'repairing the world', and it involves all of one's actions: how one treats fellow human beings, works, plays, thinks and interacts with all aspects of the environment at any given moment in time. Therefore, these 'heretical' Kabbalists believed that acts which benefit God included deliberate forays into the world of sin, where the illusory nature of evil could be more readily exposed, and the sparks thereby elevated to their Source. (11)

The Lurianic Kabbalists originally intended their practice of prayer intentions, or kavvanot, as inward actions of thought designed to reintegrate the 'Divine Light' by helping to restore it to the places it had occupied before the catastrophic fall. Thus, each kavvanah (prayer) was a spiritual act demonstrating that the outward undertaking which occasioned it harmonized invisibly with the overall structure of the cosmos. (1)

With the advent of the Messiah of 1666, however, this structure changed. The change in turn led to a revaluation of the entire Lurianic Kabbalah, and on occasion both Nathan of Gaza and Abraham Cardozo, a Sabbatean Marrano prophet, went so far as to direct veiled criticisms at Isaac Luria himself. For example, Nathan of Gaza, arguably Sabbatai Zevi's closest proponent, shares some insight concerning the dramatic social changes:

In the present age it is no longer in order to read the tikkunim (part of the Kabbalah) composed by Rabbi Isaac Luria of blessed memory and his disciples, nor to meditate according to their kavvanot (prayer intentions), for the times have changed. The kavvanot of Rabbi Isaac Luria were meant for his own age, which was [like] an ordinary day of the week, whereas now it is the eve of the

Sabbath, and it is not proper to treat the Sabbath as though it were a weekday. (1)

Elsewhere Nathan of Gaza clarified his position, once more expressing his belief that they had entered into a new era and reiterating his view that religious law existing prior to Sabbatai Zevi was essentially obsolete:

My meaning is that the kavvanot (prayer intentions) discovered by our teacher Rabbi Isaac Luria, may his saintly and righteous memory be blessed, are no longer appropriate to our own time, because the raising up [of the divine worlds] has entered a new phase, so that it would be like employing kavvanot intended for a weekday on the Sabbath. Therefore, let everyone beware of using them, and likewise let none of the kavvanot or homilies or writings of Rabbi Isaac Luria be read henceforward, for they are abstruse and no living man has understood them except Rabbi Hayyim Vital, who was a disciple of the master [Isaac Luria] for several years, at the end of which he surpassed him in knowledge. (1)

In traditional Sabbatean doctrine, Zevi and his followers claimed that they could liberate the sparks of holiness hidden within what seemed to be evil. Zevi himself would perform actions that violated traditional Jewish taboos, such as eating fats that were forbidden by Jewish dietary laws and celebrating former fast days as feast days. To quote a prayer by Zevi:

Baruch atah Adonai, Elohainu Melech ha-olam; matir issurim: Blessed art thou, Lord our God, King of the Universe, who makes the forbidden things permissible. (1)

The process of redemption would remain incomplete as long as the last divine sparks (nitzotzot) of holiness and good which fell at the time of Adam's primordial sin into the impure realm of the kelipot ("shells" entrapping divine light) had not been gathered back to their source. It was therefore left to the 'Redeemer', the holiest of men, to accomplish what not even the most righteous souls in the past had been able to do: to descend through the gates of impurity into the impure realm of the kelipot and to rescue the divine sparks still imprisoned there. (1)

As soon as this task was sufficiently performed, the 'Kingdom of Evil' would collapse of itself, for its existence was made possible only by the divine sparks in its midst. The Messiah was constrained to commit "strange acts" (ma'asim zarim), of which his apostasy was the most startling; all of these, however, were necessary for the fulfillment of his mission. (11)

The psychology of the radical Sabbateans was utterly paradoxical. Essentially, its guiding principle was: whoever is as he appears cannot be a true believer. In practice, this meant that true faith could not be a faith which men publicly professed. On the contrary, the true faith must always be concealed. In fact, it was one's duty to deny it outwardly, for it was like a seed planted in the bed of the soul, and it could not grow unless it was first covered over.(8) In the formulation of Cardozo:

> It is ordained that the King Messiah don the garments of a Marrano and so go unrecognized by his fellow Jews. In a word, it is ordained that he become a Marrano like me. For this reason, accordingly, every Jew is obliged to become a Marrano. (1)

This theme of a secret, hidden, or occult identity became part of this evolving religious philosophy. In essence, a true act cannot be committed publicly, before the eyes of the world. Like the true faith, the true act was concealed, for only through concealment could it negate the falsehood of what is explicit. Through a revolution of values, what was formerly sacred became profane and what was formerly profane had become sacred. (1, 8)

Sabbatai Zevi is the most famous Jew to have become a Muslim convert, and that is what, in modern times, the term Sabbatean has come to denote. Many within Zevi's inner circle followed him into Islam, including his wife Sarah and most of his closest relatives and friends. Nathan of Gaza, the proponent closest to Zevi, who had caused Zevi to reveal himself as the Messiah, and in turn became his prophet, never followed him into Islam but remained a Jew, albeit publicly excommunicated by his Jewish brethren.(11)

It is thought by some scholars that Zevi had deeper connections with the Bektashi Sufi order. Some similarities between the Sabbatean Donmeh and Bektashi practice include the deliberate violation of kashrut/halal, ritualistic group sex or wife swapping, ecstatic singing or chanting, mystical Kabbalah, and belief in an occult (hidden) reading of Torah/Quran. (5)

After Sabbatai's death in 1676, these sects flourished and continued to indulge in wife sharing, religious sex orgies, adultery and incest. The Sabbateans in Salonika, the Dolmeh, regularly held a celebration on the twenty-second day of the Hebrew month of Adar, known as the Festival of the Lamb. They kept the exact nature of this celebration a carefully guarded secret until some of the younger members were finally prevailed upon to reveal it. (36) According to their account, the festival included intoxication and an orgiastic rite called the extinguishing of the lights, which ended in total darkness, with the religious sexual sharing of daughters and wives. From what we know of this rite, it probably came to Salonika from Izmir, for it borrowed both its name and its contents from the pagan cult of the Great Mother, which flourished in antiquity and continued to be practiced, after the general demise of the cult by a small sect of Light Extinguishers in Asia Minor under the cover of Islam.(1,27) They said that the violation of the Torah had become its fulfillment, which they illustrated by the example of a grain of wheat that rots in the earth. In other words, just as a grain of wheat must rot in the earth before it can sprout, so the deeds of the believers must become truly rotten before they could germinate the redemption. This metaphor, which appears to have been extremely popular, conveyed the whole of sectarian Sabbatean psychology in a nutshell: in the period of transition, while the redemption was still in a state of concealment, the

Torah in its explicit form must be denied, for only thus could it too become concealed and ultimately 'renewed'. (1,8,11)

Some historians maintain that many Sabbateans became followers of Hasidism, which unlike Zevi's movement, followed Halakha (Jewish law). There are well-known disputes between Rabbis accusing one another of being secret followers of Zevi, who had become much reviled in Orthodox Judaism, due to his apostasy. According to Gershom Scholem:

> Sabbateanism is the matrix of every significant movement to have emerged in the eighteenth and nineteenth century, from Hasidism, to Reform Judaism, to the earliest Masonic circles and revolutionary idealism. The Sabbatean believers felt that they were champions of a new world which was to be established by overthrowing the values of all positive religions. (1)

This insistence of the radicals on the potential holiness of sin, alienated and offended the average Jew, and caused even the believers themselves to undergo the severest of internal conflicts.(36) The Sabbateans attempted to justify it by citing, out of context, the Talmudic dictum: (Nazir 23b) transgression committed for its own sake is greater than a commandment not committed for its own sake.

The nihilistic tendencies of Sabbateanism, still relatively mild compared to what was to follow, reached a new peak in the 18th century with Sabbatai Zevi's infamous successor Jacob Frank, whose followers regularly sought redemption through infamous religious sex orgies on solstices and equinoxes.

Chapter 2

In Jerry Rabow's book, *The Untold Life Stories of 50 Jewish Messiahs,* he describes Jacob Frank's philosophy:

Although Jacob Frank was born fifty years after the death Sabbatai Zevi, he deserves to be regarded as Sabbatai's true successor. He extended the paradoxical teachings of Zevi that the coming of the messianic age had transformed sexual prohibitions of the bible into permissions and even obligations. According to Frank, engaging in sexual orgies became the means to purify the soul from its sins. Debauchery became therapy. Frank convinced his followers that the only way for their special form of Judaism to survive was for them to outwardly become Christians, just as the Donmeh had descended into the world of Islam.(10)

Born the son of a Polish Sabbatean in 1726, Frank grew up to be a heretical Rabbi who claimed to be the reincarnation of both the self-proclaimed messiah Sabbatai Zevi, and the biblical patriarch Jacob. Frank created a new religion, now referred to as Frankism, which was instigated by the Lurian Kabbalah, and expanded on the 'redemption through sin' philosophy made popular by Zevi. (1,10,11)

JAKÓB JÓZEF ʙᴀʀᴏɴ ᴠᴏɴ FRANK - DOBRUCKI,

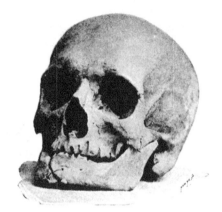

CZASZKA JAKÓBA JÓZEFA FRANKA,
Jacob Frank's actual skull

FIGURE 5

Jacob Frank asserted that God, the creator was different from the god who had revealed himself to the Isrealites. He believed the Biblical God was evil, belief widely held in Gnostic circles. Where Frank separated himself was by rejecting every moral law and commandment, and declaring that the only way to a new society was through the total destruction of the present civilization. He insisted that child sacrifice, rape, incest and the drinking of blood were perfectly acceptable and necessary religious rituals.(36)

It did not take long for the Jewish authorities in Poland to excommunicate Frank, and his followers, due to his heretical doctrines which included deification of himself and other controversial concepts such as "purification through transgression". The Frankists held annual springtime Lamb Festivals, which consisted of a celebratory dinner that included drug use, sacrifice, nudity, and the exchanging of spouses and daughters for religious sex.

Frank totally rejected the traditional interpretation of the Torah. He converted to both Islam and Catholicism. He often slept with his followers, as well as his own daughter, while preaching a doctrine that the best way to imitate God was to cross every boundary, transgress every taboo, and mix (as he claimed God did) the sacred with the profane. (36)

At the height of his popularity, approximately 50,000 Jews or ex-Jews (crypto-Jews) considered themselves his disciples. This was far less than Sabbatai Zevi, his Messianic predecessor, who had over 20 times as many followers in the prior century. Despite the smaller following, Frank's cult would grow to include some of Europe's royalty, nobility, and richest bankers.(30)

For Frank, the central theological point was the garbing of the holy in the unholy. In his pseudo-Gnostic perspective, the wholly evil world was a creation not of YHVH but of an evil creator god. And yet, God had become manifest and present in the world, thus transgressing the boundary between pure and impure. Human beings, according to Frank, to imitate God, likewise must enter into the realm of the profane.

Ewa Frank
(1754 - 1816)

FIGURE 6

Eve Frank (1754-1816) his daughter, called "The Lady" or the "Holy Matron (Mother)", served as a central figure in the sex rituals of the sect while he was still alive. After his death she continued to run the sect in Offenbach and later in Poland. (16) According to Jacob Frank:

Everything that has ever been till this day has been done so the Seed of the Jews be maintained and that the Name of Israel not be forgotten. But now there is no more need for Commandments or for Prayers, but only to listen and do and go on until we come to a certain hidden place. (36)

Gershom Scholem famously said that people will always remember Jacob Frank as one of the most frightening phenomena in the whole of Jewish history, and was: "a religious leader who, whether for purely self-interested motives or otherwise, was in all his actions a truly corrupt and degenerate individual."(1)

Jacob Frank himself candidly summed up his own philosophy in a single remark: "It is one thing to worship God and quite another to follow the path that I have taken."(1)

According to Frank, one had to free oneself of all laws, conventions, and religions, to adopt every conceivable attitude and to reject it, and to follow one's leader step by step into the abyss. The annihilation of every religion and positive system of beliefs was the true way he expected his believers to follow. Jacob Frank taught that in order to ascend one must first descend. In Frank's own words:

No man can climb a mountain until he has first descended to its foot. Therefore we must descend and be cast down to the bottom rung, for only then can we climb to the infinite. This is the mystic principle of Jacob's Ladder, which I have seen and which is shaped like a V... Again, I did not come into this world to lift you up but rather to cast you down to the bottom of the abyss. Further than this it is impossible to descend, nor can one ascend again by virtue of one's own strength, for only the Lord can raise one up from the depths by the power of His hand. (1)

Frank went on to explain that the descent into the abyss required not only the rejection of all religions and conventions, but also the commission of strange acts, which in turn demanded voluntary abasement, so that libertinism (disregard of authority), and the state of utter shamelessness, which led to a tikkun (fixing/rectification) of the soul, became one and the same thing.

To overcome these opposing powers, which are the gods of other religions, it was imperative that one be perfectly silent, even deceitful. This was the mystic principle of the burden of silence, a new version of the original Sabbatean injunction against appearing as one really was. Frank articulated this need for silence, as well as its burden:

Indeed, this is the principle of the true way itself: Just as a man who wishes to conquer a fortress does not do it by means of making a speech, but must go there himself with all his forces, so we too must go our way in silence. It is better to see than to speak, for the heart must not reveal what it knows to the mouth. We are under the burden of silence: here we must be quiet and bear what is needful, and that is why it is a burden. When a man goes from one place to another he should hold his tongue. It is the same as with a man drawing a bow: the longer he holds his breath, the further the arrow will fly. (1)

These are some of the main features of Frank's Kabbalistic interpretations and his religious nihilism. Among the Frankists, an astonishing and clear-cut ideology of Jewish territorialism developed. As stated by a Frankist writer in Prague, Israel's exile was not a consequence of its sins at all, but was part of a plan to bring about the destruction of the kelipot all over the world. As a result,even if several thousands or tens-of-thousands of Jews return to the Land of Israel, nothing would have been completed. According to the same author this new doctrine of the exile was a supposedly secret mystical principle which was hidden from all the sages until it was revealed in Poland. (1)

In his classic book, *To Eliminate the Opiate (Vol. 2)*, Rabbi Marvin S. Antelman explains where Jacob Frank's got his financing:

Frankfurt at the time was the headquarters of the Jesuit, Adam Weishaupt, founder of the Illuminati, as well as Rothschild Brothers' financial empire. This is worth repeating: Frankfurt was the birthplace of both the Illuminati and the Rothschild empire.

When Jacob Frank entered the city, the alliance between the two had already begun. Weishaupt provided the conspiratorial resources of the Jesuit Order, while the Rothschilds contributed the money. What was missing was a means to spread the agenda of the Illuminati and that the Frankists added with their network of agents throughout the Christian and Islamic worlds. Jacob Frank became instantly wealthy because he was given a nice handout by Mayer Amshel Rothschild of Frankfurt. (11)

Chapter 3

May 1, 1776 was the formal date that Adam Weishaupt officially founded the Orden der Perfektibilisten (The Order of Perfectibilists), also known as the Illuminati of Bavaria. Weishaupt was the son of a Jewish Kabbalist Rabbi in Bavaria, but educated by the Jesuits who converted him to Catholicism after his father died when he was five. He eventually became a priest, but defected and formed an alliance with Lord Meyer Rothschild who financed the Illuminati agenda.(29)

FIGURE 7

When Adam Weishaupt formed the Order of the Illuminati, he arranged the timing of key events by Kabbalistically arranging numbers in a manner which would add to numbers of greatest occult significance. For example, he chose May 1, because May, the fifth month added to the first day, equals six. Weishaupt chose 1776, because the four numbers of this year add up to 21 (1+7+7+6 = 21). Further, the sacred number 6 + 21 = 27 was another number with occult Kabbalistic "power", because it is formed by multiplying 3x9. Weishaupt carefully chose this date because he believed that even the greatest plan would be doomed to failure if it was not carried out at the most numerically advantageous time.

The long term political goals of their occult secret society called for the execution of the following plan:

1. Abolition of all monarchies and all ordered governments
2. Abolition of private property and inheritances
3. Abolition of patriotism and nationalism.
4. Abolition of family life and the institution of marriage
5. The establishment of communal education for children
6. Abolition of all religion (30)

In his book, *Shabatai Tzvi: Labor Zionism and the Holocaust*, Jewish author Barry Chamish says that:

The Rothschilds goal was to control the wealth of the planet. And the Frankist vision was the destruction of Jewish ethics to be replaced by a religion based on the exact opposite of God's intentions. When these factions blended, a bloody war against humanity, with the Jews on the front lines, erupted and it is reaching its very pinnacle at this moment. (8)

In 1777, the Illuminati began to co-operate with all the Masonic lodges (especially the Grand Orient) with the purpose of infiltrating them. Even the Duke of Brunswick, Grand Master of Germany, said in 1794 that the Illuminati controlled the Masonic lodges. In time, the Illuminati won control of every Masonic order in the world. When Weishaupt became a member of the Grand Orient, Mayer Amschel Rothschild (1743-1812), the founder of the Rothschild dynasty, provided the financial backing for the lodge, according to the British historian Nesta Webster.(27) According to Rabbi Marvin Antelman, Rothschild convinced Weishaupt to accept the Frankist doctrine, and afterward financed the Illuminati. He aimed to fulfill the Frankist plot of subverting the world's religions, and the Zionist objective of instituting a global government which would be ruled by a King from Jerusalem. (11)

In Latin, Lucifer literally means 'Light-bearer'. As its name implied, members of the Illuminati possessed the 'Light of Lucifer'. They believed that people who possessed it were truly enlightened and capable of governing. Their avowed purpose and goal was the establishment of a "Novus Ordo Seclorum" - a New World Order, or One World Government, ruled by it's capital in Jerusalem.

Mayer Rothschild summoned 12 affluent men to Frankfort, and asked them to pool their financial resources. He then presented the 25-point plan that would enable them to gain control of the wealth, natural resources and manpower of the entire world. This plan included instructions on how to preach "Liberalism" to usurp political power, initiate class warfare, dismantle and reconstruct all existing institutions, and remain invisible until the very moment when the Illuminati had gained such strength that no cunning or force can undermine it. (9,13,29) Other highlights of their plan included the use of mob psychology to control the masses. They would systematically advocate and use alcoholic liquors, drugs, moral corruption and all forms of vice to corrupt the youth. (30) In addition, they planned to use the press for propaganda to control all outlets of public information, while remaining in the shadows, clear of blame. The plan called for the masses to be made to believe that they had been the prey of criminals, and then they would restore order and to appear as the saviors. (29,30)

A key to their success was the infiltration of Freemasonry to take advantage of the Grand Orient Lodges, cloaking the true nature of their work in philanthropy. They plotted to use this influence to spread their atheistic-materialistic ideology amongst the "Goyim" (gentiles/cattle), through systematic deception, high-sounding phrases and popular slogans. Ultimate world government was the goal, through corporate monopolies, so that even the largest fortunes of the goyim ("non-Jews") will depend on them. (9,13)

There would be the all out use of economic warfare, with a combination of high taxes and unfair competition. They intended to control a sufficient police force and domestic soldiers to protect their interests. They would call this paradigm The New World Order, and eventually appoint a dictator.(29)

Fritz Springmeier, an author who is currently serving time in Federal prison, has written several books on Illuminati blood lines. In *The Illuminati Formula to Create an Undetectable Total Mind Control*, he described this global communist plan:

◇◇

There is a connection between Marxism and a group of Satanists called Frankists. One of the strongest satanic cults to take control over the Jewish population was called Sabbatianism. Jacob Frank assumed the role of leader of this group, and afterward this brand of satanism was called Frankism. (Freud's sexually obsessed theories came from Frankism.) Frank taught his followers to convert to another religion and hide behind that religion to practice their satanism. (9)

◇◇

Adam Weishaupt founded the Order of the Illuminati on approximately the same structural principles as the Jesuit Order. He had worked five years to develop, or modify, a system based on that of the Jesuits, which divided the Order into three classes (the Jesuits had four). The first class was for novices and the lesser illuminated (Minerval), the second for Freemasons (including the Scottish Knights), and the third, the mystery class, was comprised of priests, regents, magicians and a king (the Jesuits had a general). (30)

The plan for seizing power was ingeniously simple. They would make the molders of public opinion (priests, writers, officials) into obedient tools, whereupon they would, in Weishaupt's words "surround the princes". As advisers to the elite, they would influence politics in favor of the Illuminati's aims. (13)

When entering the Order, new brothers vowed: "I shall never use my position or post against another brother." Through the network of Illuminati membership, Meyer Rothschild redoubled his efforts and his banking empire became firmly entrenched throughout Europe. His sons, who became Barons in the Austrian Empire, continued to build their father's financial empire, and to expand their political influence.

In 1785, Meyer Amschel Rothschild moved his entire family to a five story dwelling he shared with the Schiff family. He died on September 19, 1812. His will spelled out specific guidelines to be followed and maintained by his descendants:

1) All important posts were to be held only by family members, and only male members were to be involved on the business end. The oldest son of the oldest son was head of the family, unless otherwise agreed upon by the rest of the family, as was the case in 1812, when the family appointed Nathan the patriarch.

2) The family was to intermarry with their own first and second cousins, to keep the fortune in the family, and to maintain the appearance of a united financial empire. This rule became less important in later generations as they refocused family goals and married into other fortunes.

3) There was never to be "any public inventory made by the courts, or otherwise, of my estate. Also, I forbid any legal action and any publication of the value of the inheritance." (30)

In 1894 a well-known Jewish author, Bernard Lazar, wrote in his book "L'Anti-semitisme", that Kabbalist Jews surrounded Weishaupt. Confiscated documents show that of 39 Illuminati holding lesser leading positions, 17 were Jews. The higher one looked into their ranks, the larger the percentage of Jews.(29)(31) There were four especially important Jews in the Illuminati leadership: Hartwig (Naphtali Herz) Wessely, Moses Mendelssohn, the banker Daniel von Itzig (1723-1799) and the businessman David Friedlander. The initiated all took a vow to eternal silence, undeviating loyalty and total submission to the Order. Each member had to promise: "I pledge to count what is best for the Order as my own best, I am ready to serve it with my personal fortune, my honour and my blood... the friends and enemies of the Order shall also become my friends and enemies." (31) Then, to ensure utmost secrecy, the group formally warned each new member:

If you are a traitor and a perjurer, then know that the brothers shall take up arms against you. Do not hope to flee or to find a place to hide. Wherever you are, shame, contempt and the wrath of the brothers shall pursue and torment you to your innermost entrails. (31)

The Order led most members to believe that the lower degrees of mystery they had reached were the highest. Few members knew about the true purpose of the Order. Many members believed themselves to be working towards the improvement of the world. They never guessed that the true, or deeper, purpose was to establish Novus Ordo Seclorum; a global program for world domination. Adam Weishaupt taught:

To some of these Freemasons we shall not even reveal that we have anything more than what the Freemasons have... All those who are not suitable for the work shall remain in the Masonic lodge and advance there without knowing anything about the additional system. (6)

In time, the Illuminati won control of every Masonic order in the world. The Illuminati moved freely within the many secret societies of the time seeking to utilize the liberal ideology of Freemasonry as a bait for those who lacked knowledge of its true purposes. (13, 29)

"All Illuminati are Freemasons but far from all Freemasons are Illuminati," stated Professors Cosandey and Renner from Munich in their testimonies in April, 1785, implying that only a minority ever reached the highest mystery degrees. Adam Weishaupt himself wrote: "The [Masonic] Lodge shall be our nursery garden. All those who are not suited to the work shall remain in the Masonic Lodge and advance in that without knowing anything of the further system. (16)

On 20 July 1785, Jakob Lanz, a priest acting as a courier for the Illuminati was hit by lightning while riding his horse and died. Police discovered a list of Illuminati members, and some compromising papers, sewn into his priest's robe. The local police found other important documents at Lanz' house, including detailed instructions for the planned French revolution. Some of the papers were addressed to the Grand Master of the Lodge Grand Orient in Paris. Everything was handed over to the Bavarian government which then issued a new ban on secret societies on the 4th August 1785. On 31 August, the government issued an order to arrest Weishaupt, and put a price on his head.(6)

The police began to look for other known members of the Order, which had successfully infiltrated many important posts in society. In Oc-

FIGURE 8

tober 1786, they searched the house of Dr Franz Xaver Zwack (Cato) in Landshut where the Illuminati kept their most important papers. The following year the police searched Baron Bassus' (Hannibal's) castle in Sandersdorf and confiscated even more papers concerning the Illuminati's conspiracy against the whole world. The Illuminati were forced to leave their lodges. Despite the ban, they continued to act as ordinary Freemasons. (30) According to Albert Pike, Freemasons, from the start, should be deliberately lied to and, mislead as to the meaning of the symbols:

◇◇

Masonry, like all the Religions, all the Mysteries, the Hermeticism and Alchemy, conceals its secrets from all except the Adepts and Sages, or the Elect, and uses false explanations and misinterpretations of its symbols to mislead those who deserve only to be mislead; to conceal the Truth, which it calls Light, from them, and to draw them away from it. Truth is not for those who are unworthy or unable to receive it, or would pervert it... So Masonry jealously conceals its secrets, and intentionally leads conceited interpreters astray. (32)

◇◇

Chapter 4

Whenever we see a pirate ship on television, in movies, or in comic books we also see an extremely ancient symbol - the skull and crossbones. This symbol, however, was not always of death or poison but instead it had another occult meaning. The official symbol of the Skull & Bones secret society is a human skull sitting atop two human bones crossed like an "X", underneath of which is the number "322". People throughout the world have speculated as to the true meaning of "322" which, according to Anthony Sutton, goes back to ancient times:

FIGURE 9

The Order is descended from a Greek fraternal society dating back to Demosthenes in 322 B.C. This has perhaps some credibility because Bones records are dated by adding 322 to the current year, i.e., records originating in 1950 are dated Anno - Demostheni 2272. (33)

◇◇

In the book, *The Holy Blood and The Holy Grail*, Baigent, Leigh and Lincoln tell the tale this way:

◇◇

A great lady of Maraclea was loved by a Templar, A Lord of Sidon; but she died in her youth, and on the night of her burial, this wicked lover crept to the grave, dug up her body and violated it.. he opened the grave.. and found a head on the leg bones of the skeleton (skull and crossbones). (7)

◇◇

What's interesting about this is that the port of Sidon was known historically as a 'nest of pirates', even being labeled as such by Constantine Porphyrogenitus (905-959 AD). Pirates famously used the skull and bones on their flags. Jolly Roger is the traditional English name for these flags. The links between the Templars and Sidon are strong: Templars were highly commercial and indeed linked to slavery; so was Sidon, as the slave trade continued there after the fall of slavery elsewhere.(39)

In Genesis, Sidon is a son of Canaan, a grandson of Noah. It is located in modern day Lebanon, known in ancient times as Phoenicia. The Phoenicians traveled far beyond the Pillars of Hercules. Greek historians recorded that they circumnavigated Africa and even had links to the British Isles. But is it possible they went much farther than that?

Most archeologists still can not explain ancient traces of drugs from the 'New World', such as cocaine and tobacco in Egyptian mummies. Perhaps the secretive Phoenicians - who jealously guarded their secret trade routes - may have been behind this mysterious, trans-Atlantic trade. In fact, it wouldn't surprise me if they were behind the false propaganda of a "flat earth" deliberately spreading fear, to steer away potential competition to what may actually have been an ancient trade monopoly.

The Templars themselves likely knew the earth was round, as the Kabbalah clearly stated it. (40)

FIGURE 10

There is an interesting story of a stone found in Brazil with etchings on it ascribed to the Phoenicians, who were said to have set sail around Africa and wound up on the shores of Brazil during the nineteenth year of the reign of King Hiram, some 500 years BC. These etchings have become known as the Paraiba Stone Inscription of Brazil, written in ancient Phoenician. The translation reads:

We are children of Canaan from Sidon of the Eastern Kingdom of Merchants and are cast, I pray, here beside a central land of mountains (with this) offered choice gift to the Most High Gods and Goddesses in year 19 of King Hiram, I pray (still) strong, from the valley of Ezion-geber of the Red Sea. Thereby (we) journeyed with 10 ships and we were at sea together assuredly two years around the land of Ham. We were separated by the hand of Baal and no longer remained among our companions, I pray, we have come here, 12 men and 3 women at this new land. Devoted, I make, even whom men of wealth bow the knee, a pledge to the Most High Gods and Goddesses (with) sure hope.(46)

◇◇◇

Although plenty of skeptics will say the story is just a hoax, there is also no shortage of independent scholars who defend the sea-faring capabilities of these ancient Phoenician pirates. From *The Phoenician Theory:*

◇◇◇

Ibarra Grasso has identified two Phoenician ships on the centre slabs of the temple of Sechim, in the Casma Valley, on the coast of Peru. These ruins are generally considered to be some three thousand years old. Even more extraordinary are the discoveries made by Bernardo Silva Ramos. (Ramos) spent over twenty years in the Amazon rainforest... photographing and copying 2,800 stone inscriptions, identifying the majority of them as Phoenician and others as Greek. The oriental scholar Lienhardt Delekat has established that the characters on the Paraíba Stone are of Canaanite origin . The stone, which broke into four pieces after it was discovered on a plantation, totally disappeared, but copies of the inscription were made before this occurred. It was discovered on September 11, 1872 and might well be proof that Phoenician sailors reached Brazil two thousand years before the official discovery of America. Lienhardt Delekat's translation reads as follows: We are children of Canaan, from the city of Sidon. We are a nation of traders. Our ship is beached on this far-off mountainous coast and we want to make a sacrifice to the gods and goddesses. In the 19th year of Irma's reign, we set sail from Ezlon Geber across the Red Sea, with ten ships. (41)

◇◇◇

The Phoenicians had a strong presence in North Africa and on the Iberian peninsula, particularly at the Pillars of Hercules and Gibraltar. Archaeologists have found a temple to Hercules at the entrance to the Mediterranean in what is now called Gorham's Cave. Many researchers believe that the twin columns Boaz and Jachin, from the Phoenician-designed Solomon's Temple, are in fact a representation of the Pillars of Hercules, a secret symbol of the Phoenicians planted in the heart of Jerusalem itself. (42)

A notorious secret society at Yale University goes by the name of Skull and Bones. The alumni organization that owns the property and oversees the organization is officially called the Russell Trust Association, named after General William Huntington Russell who was one of the co-founders of the association in 1832, along with Alphonso Taft; father of President William H. Taft. At first, the society held its meetings in hired halls. Then in 1856, the "Tomb", a vine-covered, windowless, brown-stone hall was constructed, where to this day the "Bonesmen" hold their strange, occultist initiation rites and meet bi-weekly. On September 29, 1876, a group calling itself "The Order of File and Claw" broke into the Skull and Bones' holy of holies. In the "Tomb," they found lodge-room 324 "fitted up in black velvet, even the walls being covered with the material." Upstairs was lodge-room 322, "the 'sanctum sanctorium' of the temple, furnished in red velvet" with a pentagram on the wall. In the hall, were "pictures of the founders of Bones at Yale, and of members of the Society in Germany, when the chapter was established here in 1832." (29)

Dr. Cathy Burns is author of the book, *Masonic and Occult Symbols Illustrated*, and her interpretation of the skull and cross-bones is one that I suspect most people in the general public are unfamiliar with:

The sign Constantine referred to was NOT a Christian cross, but a kind of 'X'... In modern magic, it is the sign of the slain and risen Egyptian god, Osiris (another version of the 'slain and risen' Hiram Abif).(34)

During the Templars' sojourn in the Holy Land, they became acquainted with the Kabbalah and learned the mysterious teachings of various other Jewish and Sufi sects. In Hermetic Kabbalah, the skull and bones relate to the Chi-Rho, symbolizing time, death, and rebirth. According to Egyptologist Sir Flinders Petrie, the Chi-Rho was the emblem of the Egyptian god, Horus. On the coinage during and after Constantine's death, we see the Chi-Rho, underlined with the serpent, a symbol used throughout time, and especially by the Gnostics and alchemists, for wisdom and the enlightenment process.

FIGURE 11

An identical symbol to the Chi-Rho has been found inscribed on rocks dating from 2,500 BC in Sumer (ancient Mesopotamia), and was interpreted as a combination of the two Sun-symbols.(35) Their system also incorporated the Assassins' mysticism and perverse practices; their Christian faith had given way to secret occultist rituals and Black Magic rites. These families were hiding behind a Christian facade. In his books, author David Livingstone traces the genealogies of these ancient occult bloodlines, which include the Rothschilds, the Hapsburgs, the Sinclairs, the Stuarts, the Merovingians, the Lusignans, and the Windsors. (26) In Livingstone's words:

The Illuminati Order was preceded in the 1500's in Spain by the 'Alumbrados,' a Christian heresy started by crypto Jews called "Marranos." The founder of the Jesuit Order, Ignatius of Loyola, was a Marrano/Alumbrado. Thus when people today argue whether it is the Jesuits or Zionists who are responsible for our troubles, they are really talking about the same beast. Kabbalist Rabbi Isaac Luria, a follower of Loyola's (the crypto-Jew founder of the Jesuits), enunciated the principle that they must work actively to bring about prophesy, i.e. redemption through the coming of the Messiah and the rule of the Illuminati. This meant "manipulating the course of fate through the use of magic, and finally, of preparing the necessary political and moral circumstances to receive [the Messiah i.e. Antichrist's] coming, that is a New World Order. (26)

Chapter 5

In an infamous letter to New York agents in 1863, Rothschild banker John Sherman characterized the Illuminati's proposal for a national bank to finance their occult agenda in these terms:

> The few who understand the system will either be so interested in its profits, or so dependent on its favors, that there will be no opposition from that class.. The great body of the people, mentally incapable of comprehending, will bear its burden without complaint, and perhaps without even suspecting that the system is inimical (contrary) to their interests. (29)

According to Edith Starr Miller, the Rothschild syndicate included Jewish financiers such as Daniel Itzig, Friedlander, the Goldsmids and Moses Mocatta. She states that:

> The goals of the Illuminati (Communism and the NWO) were the destruction of Christianity, monarchies, nation-states (in favor of

their world government or "internationalism"), the abolition of family ties and marriage by means of promoting homosexuality and promiscuity; the end of inheritance and private property; and the suppression of any collective identity in the spurious name of "universal human brotherhood," i.e. "diversity." (12)

Jewish author Dr. Henry Makow's controversial book, *Illuminati: The Cult That Hijacked the World*, offers a straight forward summary of the Illuminati agenda, and the unsuspecting populace that is being manipulated and exploited:

Most Jews are unaware of the Illuminati agenda. They are manipulated and compromised like everyone else. The Illuminati hides behind the skirts of ordinary Jews. The cult that hijacked the world is the tiny nucleus of Kabbalistic bankers and Masons based in London and directed by the House of Rothschild.. Judaism has been hijacked.. Originally Judaism was based on Moses' vision of God as a universal moral force. Judaism today is based on the Talmud, which consists of the interpretations of 'sages' (Pharisees) during the Babylonian exile 586 BC to 1040 AD. Generally speaking, the Talmud contradicts the spirit of Moses and takes precedence over the Old Testament. The 'secret society' appears to be the organizational model for Judaism as well as Freemasonry, Zionism and Communism (which are Masonic orders). Essentially, the leadership deceives and manipulates the membership with idealistic-sounding goals. Only those corruptible (and blackmail-able) are let in on the true agenda and allowed to rise. (13)

According to Dr. Makow, these elite bankers control the world's major corporations, mainstream media, intelligence agencies, think tanks, foundations and federally funded Universities that are responsible for suppressing the truth.(13) He contends that the promotion of feminism and favoritism to non-white minorities is part of an agenda to undermine the European heterosexual Christian character of Western society. So is mass immigration and interracial marriage, which he claims are designed to degrade and remove any unified opposition. In his view, most of what passes for modern culture (TV, movies, literature, punditry etc.) and politics are propaganda and well crafted social engineering. (13) For example, opprobrium for "sexism" and "racism" are actually designed to undermine gender and race; "guilt" is a huge weapon for them. Dr. Makow continues:

> Today British, American and Zionist imperialism manifest the banker agenda for "world government" through the destruction of religion, nation, race and family. This imperialism does not express the interests or wishes of ordinary English, American or Jewish people who are being colonized themselves. The Rockefeller and Morgan empires are part of the central banking cartel. At the highest level, all intelligence agencies (MI-6, CIA, Mossad, KGB) answer to this cartel, not to their national government. (13)

Dr. Henry Makow, who candidly refers to himself as an assimilated Jew, claims that the Babylonian Talmud and heretical interpretations of the Jewish Kabbalah undoubtedly contribute to anti-Semitism. David Bay, of Cutting Edge Ministry, mirrors this sentiment:

> The Kabbalah is the keystone of all Western occult thought and practice today. It is the cornerstone of belief for all Illumined Ones [Masters of the Illuminati] and is hostile to non-Kabbalistic Jews. (13)

In her book, *The Jewish Religion: Its Influence Today* (formerly titled *The Plot against Christianity*), author and conspiracy researcher Elizabeth

Dilling writes: "The attitude resulting from such teachings has been resented by non-Jews in all countries and centuries. Such resentment, however, is always portrayed by Jews as 'persecution' of the Jews." (14)

The Illuminati, which consist of the descendants of the Knights Templar and their allies the Kabbalist-globalist banking families, such as the Rothschild dynasty, have always idealized the Greek philosophers, all while practicing aberrated forms of Frankist-Luciferianism (hardcore Satanism). It was none other than Masonic leader, Albert Pike, who admitted that Freemasons worship Lucifer (Light-bearer) or Satan:

The true name of Satan, the Kabbalist say, is that of Yahveh reversed; for Satan is not a black god, but the negation of God Lucifer the Light-bearer! Strange and mysterious name to give to the Spirit of Darkness! Lucifer, the Son of the morning! It is he who bears the light Doubt it not! (17)

The Kabbalah depicts the achievement of universal harmony in terms of facilitating the sexual union of male and female deities. It preaches that "arousal below provokes arousal above." It provides the basis for the Illuminati sex cult reflected in the ancient solar symbol, the dot in a circle, which in the occult also symbolizes the penis and vagina.(36) Some people may believe that "free sex" is "progressive", with modern roots stemming from the sexual and counter-cultural revolutions of the 1960's. In fact, the Sabbatean sects have fully indulged themselves in ritualistic wife sharing, drug use, sex orgies, adultery and incest for more than 350 years. Sexual abandon characterizes Communist philosophy, a direct outgrowth of Sabbatean-Frankism. Jacob Frank himself pimped his beautiful wife to recruit influential men. The Communist Party used its female members in the same way. Adam Weishaupt, the co-founder of the Illuminati, got his sister-in-law pregnant. Their "Illuminated" secret societies performed religious ritualistic sex rites, mirroring those found in the teachings of Socratic 'communism' of ancient Greece, which were later modernized and popularized by the teachings of Aleister Crowley and his Sex Magick (Crowley spelled "Magick" with a 'K' to differentiate it from the magic of stage illusionists). (13)

FIGURE 12

These sex cults were very similar to the Socratic ideal, which held all things in common, including their wives and children, especially for sexual purposes. This is the real reason why the Athenians convicted Socrates of corrupting the youth, and forced him to drink "hemlock" (poison). (37)

The Illuminati bankers created Communism to harness the working class to their program of a comprehensive world dictatorship ("globalization"). The Illuminati and Communists are Masonic secret societies that celebrate the same anniversary, May 1, 1776 and share the same Satanic symbols. (13)

George Wilhelm Friedrich Hegel was a 19th century German philosopher who devised a particular dialectic, or, method of argument for resolving disagreements. His method of arriving at the truth by the exchange of logical arguments is a system of thought process still in use to this day.

To put it simply, Hegelianism dictates that the human mind cannot understand anything unless it can be split into two polar opposites: Good/Evil, Right/Wrong, Left/Right, etc.(26)

For example, when people talk about two political parties, Labor or Liberal, what they are actually referring to, without realizing it, is a thesis and antithesis based off the Hegelian Dialectic. The only real debate that occurs is just within the minor differences between those two parties. Nothing is said or done about the issues that neither left nor right are discussing.(29)

Another form of the Hegelian Dialectic is problem, reaction, then solution. Almost all major events in history employ the Hegelian Dialectic: 'Problem', manufacture a crisis or take advantage of one already in place in order to get the desired crisis, followed by 'Reaction' of public outcry, whereby the public demands a 'Solution' which has been predetermined from the beginning. Denis Healey, the former British Secretary of Defense once said: "World events do not occur by accident. They are made to happen, whether it is to do with national issues or commerce; most of them are staged and managed by those who hold the purse string." (29)

In an article titled, "British Freemasonry Covets Israel", Jewish-Israeli author Barry Chamish claims that there would be no modern state of Israel without British Freemasonry:

In the 1860s, the British-Israelite movement was initiated from within Freemasonry. Its goal was to establish a Jewish-Masonic state in the Turkish province of Palestine.. Initially, British Jewish Masonic families like the Rothschilds and Montefiores provided the capital to build the infrastructure for the anticipated wave of immigration. However, luring the Jews to Israel was proving difficult. They liked European life too much to abandon it. So Europe was to be turned into a nightmare for the Jews. (8)

In 1891, the "Labour Leader" newspaper of Britain published the following statement on the subject of the Rothschilds:

This blood-sucking crew has been the cause of untold mischief and misery in Europe during the present century, and has piled up its prodigious wealth chiefly through fomenting wars between States which ought never to have quarrelled. Whenever there is trouble in Europe, wherever rumours of war circulate and men's minds are distraught with fear of change and calamity you may be sure that a hook-nosed Rothschild is at his games somewhere near the region of the disturbance. (30)

Comments like this worried the Rothschilds, and towards the end of the 1800s they purchased the Reuters news agency so they could have some control of the media. Furthermore, the Rothschilds had control of three European news agencies, Wolff (est. 1849) in Germany, Reuters (est. 1851) in England, and Havas (est. 1835) in France. (30)

In 1913 Jacob Schiff set up the Anti Defamation League (ADL) in the United States. He formed this organization to slander anyone who questioned or challenged the Rothschild global conspiracy as anti-semitic. From around that time on, the media rarely reported on the Rothschilds, because they own the media.(30)

Congress voted on the Rothschild's Federal Reserve Act on December 22nd, 1913, between the hours of 1:30 and 4:30 AM. Woodrow Wilson, the president who signed the law that created the Federal Reserve, later sounded like he had regretted the decision when he wrote:

A great industrial nation is controlled by its system of credit. Our system of credit is privately concentrated. The growth of the nation, therefore, and all our activities are in the hands of a few men. [W]e have come to be one of the worst ruled, one of the most completely controlled and dominated governments in the civilized world no longer a government by free opinion, no longer a government by conviction and the vote of the majority, but a government by the opinion and the duress of small groups of dominant men. (30)

◇◇

Chapter 6

In 1917, Chaim Weizmann became president of the British Zionist Federation. He worked with the United Kingdom's Foreign Secretary, Arthur James Balfour, to obtain the milestone Balfour Declaration, which stated in writing that in exchange for bringing America into the war against Germany the British would give Palestine to the Rothschild Zionists: "His Majesty's government view with favor the establishment in Palestine of a national home for the Jewish people, and will use their best endeavors to facilitate the achievement of this object." (11)

The press published the letter one week later, and the "Balfour Declaration" was later incorporated into the peace treaty with the Ottoman Empire and the Mandate for Palestine. The original document is kept at the British Library. The reason that America entered WW1, directly leading to the defeat and destruction of Germany, was due to a formal agreement between Britain and Mr. Rothschild, which promised Palestine as a new Jewish homeland in exchange for America's entry into the war.

The Versailles peace conference, held in 1919, decided reparations that the Germans needed to pay to the victors following the end of the first world war. A delegation of 117 Zionists, headed up by Bernard Baruch,

PALESTINE FOR THE · JEWS.

OFFICIAL SYMPATHY.

Mr. Balfour has sent the following letter to Lord Rothschild in regard to the establishment of a national home in Palestine for the Jewish people :—

I have much pleasure in conveying to you, on behalf of his Majesty's Government, the following declaration of sympathy with Jewish Zionist aspirations which has been submitted to and approved by the Cabinet :—

His Majesty's Government view with favour the establishment in Palestine of a national home for the Jewish people, and will use their best endeavours to facilitate the achievement of this object, it being clearly understood that nothing shall be done which may prejudice the civil and religious rights of existing non-Jewish communities in Palestine, or the rights and political status enjoyed by Jews in any other country.

I should be grateful if you would bring this declaration to the knowledge of the Zionist Federation.

FIGURE 13

brought up the subject of Palestine. At this point, the defeated Germans realized why America had turned against them politically and militarily, and under whose influence, namely the Rothschilds. (8, 9, 30)

The Germans, naturally, felt the Zionist had betrayed them. This was because, at the time the Rothschilds made this deal with Britain for Palestine, Germany was the friendliest country in the world towards the Jews. The German Emancipation Edict of 1822 guaranteed Jews in Germany all the civil rights enjoyed by Germans. Germany was also the only country in Europe which did not place restrictions on Jews, even giving them refuge when they had to flee Russia after their first attempted Communist coup failed there in 1905.(30)

Born in 1890, Benjamin H. Freedman was a successful Jewish businessman of New York City who was at one time the principal owner of the Woodbury Soap Company. Starting in 1945, he spent the great preponderance of his considerable fortune, at least 2.5 million dollars, exposing the tyranny which had enveloped the United States. Mr. Freedman was personally acquainted with Bernard Baruch, Samuel Untermyer, Woodrow Wilson, Franklin Roosevelt, Joseph Kennedy, John F. Kennedy, and many more movers and shakers of our times. The following shortened excerpt is from a speech given by Mr. Freedman before a packed audience at the Willard Hotel in Washington, D.C. in 1961:

World War I broke out in the summer of 1914. Within two years Germany had won that war: not alone won it nominally, but won it actually. The German submarines, which were a surprise to the world, had swept all the convoys from the Atlantic Ocean, and Great Britain stood there without ammunition for her soldiers, stood there with one week's food supply facing her, and after that, starvation. At that time, the French army had mutinied. They lost 600,000 of the flower of French youth in the defense of Verdun on the Somme. The Russian army was defecting. They were picking up their toys and going home, they didn't want to play war anymore. And the Italian army had collapsed. Not a shot had been fired on the German soil. Not an enemy soldier had crossed the border into Germany. And yet, here was Germany offering England peace terms. They offered England a negotiated peace on what the lawyers call a status quo ante basis. That means: "Let's call the war off, and let everything be as it was before the war started." England, in the summer of 1916 was considering that. Seriously! They had no choice. It was either accepting this negotiated peace that Germany was magnanimously offering them, or going on with the war and being totally defeated.

While that was going on, the Zionists in Germany went to the British War Cabinet and - I am going to be brief because this is a long story, but I have all the documents to prove any statement that I make if anyone here is curious, or doesn't believe what I'm saying is at all possible - the Zionists went to the British war cabinet and they said: "Look here. You can yet win this war. You don't have to give up. You don't have to accept the negotiated peace offered to you now by Germany. You can win this war if the United States will come in as your ally." The United States was not in the war at that time. We were fresh; we were young; we were rich; we were powerful. They [Zionists] told England: "We will guarantee to bring the United States into the war as your ally, to fight with you on

your side, if you will promise us Palestine after you win the war."
In other words, they made this deal: "We will get the United States
into this war as your ally. The price you must pay us is Palestine
after you have won the war and defeated Germany." Now England
had as much right to promise Palestine to anybody, as the United States would have to promise Japan to Ireland for any reason
whatsoever. It's absolutely absurd that Great Britain - that never
had any connection or any interest or any right in what is known
as Palestine - should offer it as coin of the realm to pay the Zionists
for bringing the United States into the war. However, they made
that promise, in October of 1916. And shortly after that the United States, which was almost totally pro-German - totally pro-German - because the newspapers here were controlled by Jews, the
bankers were Jews, all the media of mass communications in this
country were controlled by Jews, and they were pro-German because their people, in the majority of cases came from Germany,
and they wanted to see Germany lick the Czar. At that time, everything changed, like the traffic light that changes from red to green.
Where the newspapers had been all pro-German, where they'd
been telling the people of the difficulties that Germany was having
fighting Great Britain commercially and in other respects, all of a
sudden the Germans were no good. They were villains. They were
Huns. They were shooting Red Cross nurses. They were cutting off
babies' hands. And they were no good. Well, shortly after that, Mr.
Wilson declared war on Germany.

That's how the United States got into the war. We had no more right
to be in it than we have to be on the moon tonight instead of in this
room. We went in there - we were railroaded into it - if I can be
vulgar, we were suckered into - that war merely so that the Zionists
of the world could obtain Palestine. Now, that is something that
the people in the United States have never been told. They never
knew why we went into World War One. After we got into the war,
the Zionists went to Great Britain and they said: "Well, we per-

formed our part of the agreement. Let's have something in writing that shows that you are going to keep your bargain and give us Palestine after you win the war." The Balfour Declaration was Great Britain's promise to pay the Zionists what they had agreed upon as a consideration for getting the United States into the war. The United States went in the war. The United States crushed Germany. We went in there, and it's history.

Now, when the war was ended, and the Germans went to Paris, to the Paris Peace Conference in 1919, there were 117 Jews there, as a delegation representing the Jews, headed by Bernard Baruch. I was there: I ought to know. Now what happened? The Jews at that peace conference, when they were cutting up Germany and parceling out Europe to all these nations that claimed a right to a certain part of European territory, the Jews said, "How about Palestine for us?" And they produced, for the first time to the knowledge of the Germans, this Balfour Declaration. So the Germans, for the first time realized, "Oh, that was the game! That's why the United States came into the war." And the Germans for the first time realized that they were defeated, they suffered this terrific reparation that was slapped onto them, because the Zionists wanted Palestine and they were determined to get it at any cost.

When the Germans realized this, they naturally resented it. Up to that time, the Jews had never been better off in any country in the world than they had been in Germany. The Jews were doing very well in Germany. No question about that. Now, the Germans felt: "Well, that was quite a sellout." That's how the Germans felt towards these Jews. "We've been so nice to them"; and from 1905 on, when the first Communist revolution in Russia failed, and the Jews had to scramble out of Russia, they all went to Germany. And Germany gave them refuge. And they were treated very nicely. And here they sold Germany down the river for no reason at all other than they wanted Palestine as a so-called "Jewish commonwealth." The Jews themselves admitted that. It wasn't that the Germans in

1919 discovered that a glass of Jewish blood tasted better than Coca-Cola or Muenschner Beer. There was no religious feeling. There was no sentiment against those people merely on account of their religious belief. It was all political. Nobody cared in Germany whether a Jew went home and pulled down the shades and said "Shema' Yisrael" or "Our Father." No one cared in Germany any more than they do in the United States. Now this feeling that developed later in Germany was due to one thing: that the Germans held the Jews responsible for their crushing defeat, for no reason at all, because World War One was started against Germany for no reason for which they [Germans] were responsible. They were guilty of nothing. When Germany realized that the Jews were responsible for her defeat, they naturally resented it. But not a hair on the head of any Jew was harmed. Not a single hair. Now, the Jews sort of tried to keep the lid on this fact. They didn't want the world to really understand that they had sold out Germany, and that the Germans resented that. (44)

This is not taught in any state or federally funded schools. This was, however, THE great betrayal that Hitler always talked about in his well-received speeches, even long before he had any political power. This is what attracted the German public to him, not because they were racist: Hitler's driver was a Jew, and so was his cook. German hostility and resentment towards organized Jewry and Freemasonry was not based on Aryan superiority, it was a reaction to on a covert Masonic conspiracy.

Forces Occultes (Occult Forces - subtitled "The mysteries of Freemasonry unveiled for the first time on the screen") is a French film produced in 1943 during occupied France, by an ex-Freemason who, after the war, was <u>executed</u> for making it. The film recounts the life of a young politician who joins the Freemasons. Here is the Institute for Historical Review's (IHR) description of the film:

This 1943 French production is perhaps the most important anti-Masonic feature film ever made. It tells the story of a young member of the French parliament who joins a Freemason lodge at the urging of colleagues. Although made with German encouragement and support, it nonetheless reflected broad French sentiment. After France's 'liberation', the film's director, producer and screenplay writer were severely punished (imprisoned) for their role in this production. Director Jean Many (Paul Riche), a former Freemason, was sentenced to death, and executed. With English subtitles. (38)

FIGURE 14

Forces Occultes was the last film Paul Riche directed before his unjust execution. The total running time is only around 50 minutes and the film is available to watch online for free. (38)

Chapter 7

We are all familiar with the story of Hitler that the Rothschild controlled mainstream media would like the world to believe. Hitler has been made out to be the most evil person to have ever lived, by starting needless wars and slaughtering millions of innocent people. This same story has been echoed throughout Hollywood for decades, and by now it's safe to say billions of dollars have been spent to convince two post-WW2 generations of this black and white, good vs evil perspective about the Nazi regime. What if it isn't entirely accurate?

After investigating the work of others who have documented history in an unbiased fashion, as well as those who have interviewed people who closely worked and lived alongside Hitler, I believe that there is strong evidence to suggest that what we've been told is extremely inaccurate. When Hitler came to power, the German people had no work, no money and were starving as a result of the cruel and brutal reparations imposed on Germany after WW1. A wheelbarrow full of 100 billion-mark banknotes could not buy a loaf of bread at the time, and many Germans were living in shacks after countless homes and farms had been seized by Rothschild/Rockefeller-controlled banks. In his 1967 book, The Magic of Money, Hitler's Reichsbank president, Dr. Hjalmar Horace Greeley Schacht, let out the big secret:

◇◇◇

The mark's dramatic devaluation began soon after the Reichsbank was "privatized," or delivered to private investors.(45)

◇◇◇

In other words, the German government was not responsible for the post-war hyperinflation, but rather the privately owned central bank in Germany, and its monopoly it had over the creation of money. Germany's economy was crashed and devastated by bankers, that is, until Hitler arrived.

When Adolf Hitler's period as Chancellor of Germany began, he refused to play ball with the Rockefeller-Rothschild rules, and instead issued Germany's own currency known as Reichsmarks, which were debt free and uncontrollable by international financial interests. Hitler fixed the corrupt, debt-based financial system by completely thwarting the international banking cartels, resulting in Germany printing its own currency, instead of borrowing it on interest from a Rothschild bank (which is what is currently

FIGURE 15

in place in America under the Federal Reserve, or the FED). Hitler lifted Germany out of the heinous economic depression which was imposed on it, ushering in a decade of self-determined growth and prosperity.(29,30) Germany started offering completely debt-free finance for constructing new roads, bridges, dams, canals, port facilities, and much needed repair of public and private buildings. None of the public money that Nazi Germany issued owed any interest to the International Banksters. As Hitler said, "For every Mark issued, we required the equivalent of a Mark's worth of work done, or goods produced." The unemployment problem had been solved within only two years, and Germany was back on its feet. It's been claimed, that Hitler's success in reviving his nation's economy was based on government spending for rearmament. This is a myth. As the renowned British historian A.J.P. Taylor noted:

Germany's economic recovery, which was complete by 1936, did not rest on rearmament; it was caused mainly by lavish expenditure on public works, particularly on motor roads, and this public spending stimulated private spending also, as [British economist John Maynard] Keynes had said it would.. while nearly everyone else in Europe expected a great war, Hitler was the one man who neither expected nor planned for it. (43)

If America nationalized their currency as Hitler did for Germany, they would effectively sever all ties with international bankers, the manipulation of their government and economy would cease, and they would live debt-free. Just as Hitler issued debt-free currency for Germany, Abraham Lincoln setup an interest free banking system in the United States when he was President, and he was murdered for it. Former US president Andrew Jackson issued interest-free currency, and two shots were fired at his head in an assassination attempt (the shots misfired and he survived). John F. Kennedy issued interest-free currency during his presidency, and met an untimely demise.

In his 1976 book, *The Twelve-Year Reich,* author R. Grunberger stated that there were significant drops in the rates of murder, robbery, theft, embezzlement and petty larceny during the Hitler years. Many foreigners were impressed by the improved outlook and health of Germans, including Sir Arnold Wilson, a British M.P. who visited Germany seven times after Hitler came to power. Wilson wrote:

Infant mortality has been greatly reduced and is considerably inferior to that in Great Britain. Tuberculosis and other diseases have noticeably diminished. The criminal courts have never had so little to do and the prisons have never had so few occupants. It is a pleasure to observe the physical aptitude of the German youth. Even the poorest persons are better clothed than was formerly the case, and their cheerful faces testify to the psychological improvement that has been wrought within them. (47)

A prime philosophy of Germany at the time was that all citizens should share the same standard of living. With this in mind, Nazi Germany boasted one of the largest public welfare programs in history with the slogan "None shall starve nor freeze". Every year, high-ranking Nazi's and citizens would take to the streets to collect charity for the unfortunate, which generated a feeling of comradeship toward those in need.

Chapter 8

The very first public mention of the word holocaust, in regards to WW2, came as early as 1936 from the leader of Labor Zionism, Chaim Weizmann, while addressing the World Zionist Congress. Weizmann, who would later become Israel's first President, in 1936 made the following dreadful pronouncement: "Perhaps only 2 million Jews will survive the upcoming Holocaust, (yes, he used that word) but they will be strong and good for the Land of Israel. The rest will be blown into the dust pile of history." (20)

The term "holocaust" is too often used without regard to its true meaning. Rabbi Marvin Antelman states that well before World War Two, the religious term meant "burnt offering", as in sacrifice (11). He quotes Bruno Bettelheim who said: "Calling the most callous, most brutal, most horrid, most heinous mass murder a 'burnt offering' is a sacrilege, a profanation of God and man." (11)

FIGURE 16

61

Whose sacrifice was it? For what purpose? Obviously, it had something to do with the Sabbatean-Frankist occult political agenda. According to Jewish author, Henry Makow, every time we use that word, we unwittingly join in their sacrilege. (13)

In his book published in 2005, *Shabtai Tzvi, Labor Zionism and the Holocaust*, Israeli author Barry Chamish poses a sensitive question, then offers an answer hardly ever discussed in the mainstream media or academia: "In 1932, how many organizations in Germany represented German Jewry? Over 250. In 1933, how many? One, and one only; Labour Zionism." (8)

Rothschild money and Jesuit power initiated the so-called Enlightenment. The final aim of the movement was to establish a Sabbatean-Frankist state in the historical land of the Jews. To foment the idea, life had to become so intolerable for Europe's Jews, that escape to Palestine would appear the best option. But was this plan a conspiracy theory or is this conspiracy a documented fact?

FIGURE 17

Theador Herzl, the father of modern Zionism, claimed that the establishment of a "Jewish" state would cure anti-Semitism, but he also **promoted** anti-Semitism to further his cause. In his published diary, Herzl boldly stated: "It would be an excellent idea to call in respectable, accredited anti-Semites as liquidators of property.. The anti-Semites will become our most dependable friends, the anti-Semitic countries our allies." (21)

The Israeli Historian Benny Morris described how Herzl foresaw and calculated the covert ways in which anti-Semitism could be harnessed and exploited, in order to further expedite the realization of the political goals of Zionism. He stated that:

Herzl regarded Zionism's triumph as inevitable, not only because life in Europe was ever more untenable for Jews, but also because it was in Europe's interests to rid the Jews and relieved of anti-Semitism: The European political establishment would eventually be persuaded to promote Zionism. Herzl recognized that anti-Semitism would be harnessed to his own Zionist purposes. (22)

According to historian Christopher Jon Bjerknes, Jewish support was the only thing lacking in the Rothschilds' plan to establish a world government in Jerusalem, with a Rothschild ruling as king:

They could bankrupt Egypt and Turkey. They could bring Russia to ruins. They could buy Jewish ne'er-do-wells. They could even buy the Pope but the only way to force Jews in large numbers to Palestine was to put Hitler and Stalin in power and persecute Jews on a massive and unprecedented scale. (25)

Jewish author Barry Chamish, who in the Summer of 1982 fought in the Lebanon war for the Israeli Defense Forces, and whose Grandparents died in a concentration camp in Poland, published in his book that:

We now jump to 1933. Less than 1% of the German Jews support Zionism. Many tried to escape from Naziism by boat to Latin and North American ports but the international diplomatic order was to turn them back. Any German Jew who rejected Palestine would be shipped back to his death. (8)

By 1934, the majority of German Jews got the message and turned to the only Jewish organization allowed by the Nazis, the Labour Zionists.

For confirmation of the conspiracy between them and Hitler's regime, read *The Transfer Agreement* by Edwin Black, *Perfidy* by Ben Hecht or *The Scared And The Doomed* by Jacob Nurenberger. According to Chamish, the deal cut worked something like this: "The German Jews would first be indoctrinated into Bolshevism in Labour Zionism camps and then, with British approval, transferred to Palestine." (8)

Under the 1935 Nuremberg Laws, only two flags were permitted in Nazi Germany: One was the swastika, the other was the blue and white banner of Zionism. According to Lenni Brenner's book, *Zionism in the Age of Dictators*, the Zionist party was the only other political party in Nazi Germany to enjoy a measure of freedom. Zionists and Nazis had a common interest that developed into a formal partnership: making Jews go to Palestine. (30)

The pro-eugenics Labour Zionists got the Jews they wanted (by training them in farming in NAZI camps), and let the millions of orthodox religious Jews (the ones against political Rothschild Zionism) and other non-Frankists perish in Europe, while their wealth was liquidated and transferred to the Labour Zionists (see The Transfer Agreement). (19)

While non-Zionist European Jews were in mortal danger, Zionist leaders in America deliberately provoked and enraged Hitler. They began in 1933 by initiating their worldwide boycott of Nazi goods. Chaim Weizmann, the Zionist Chief and later first President of Israel said: "Every nation has its dead in its fight for its homeland. The suffering under Hitler are our dead."(20)

Rabbi Moshe Shonfeld accuses the Rothschild Zionists of collaborating in the Nazi slaughter of European Jewry directly and indirectly. He makes these charges in his book, *Holocaust Victims Accuse*, which was published in 1977. Rabbi Shonfeld calls the Zionists "war criminals" for usurping the leadership of the Jewish people, betraying them to be slaughtered, and then reaping the moral capital from their own treachery. He states:

⟡⟡

The Zionist approach that Jewish blood is the anointing oil needed for the wheels of the Jewish state is not a thing of the past. It remains operable to this very day. (19)

⟡⟡

In a famous statement, Georgetown University professor Carol Quigley, an insider who was Bill Clinton's mentor, said: "The central banker plan is nothing less than to establish a world system, to dominate the political system of each country." (15)

By 1940, publications owned by the central bankers and their front men included The New York Herald Tribune, The New York Times, PM, The Chicago Sun, The Cowles Group (Look), Time Life, The Washington Post and the Baltimore Sun.

In his book *Crimes and Mercies*, James Bacque describes how he confronted New York Times reporter Drew Middleton with evidence that, after the war, the U.S. starved to death over one million German POWs. Bacque writes:

⟡⟡

What Middleton told me basically was that, yes, he had lied in 1945 and no, it did not matter to him or the 'New York Times' if I exposed this. Middleton's sense of security, his sense of the New York Times' power, took my breath away.. But worse than that, Middleton did not care about this atrocity.. the New York Times witnessed it, then denied that it happened. And has gone on denying it into the 1990's. (23)

⟡⟡

Bacque estimates that, during the Allied Occupation (1946-1950) an additional eight to twelve million Germans were deliberately starved to death. The war did not end in 1945. For five additional years, Germany suffered "physical and psychic trauma unparalleled in history." Red Army soldiers raped up to two million German women during the last six months of the Second World War, around 100,000 of them in Berlin. They also raped

Russian women released from German labour camps. (23) We live in a Feminist era. Have you seen any movies about these women? Outlined in, The Rothschilds, Winston Churchill and the Final Solution, Clifford Shack states that:

Through infiltration, stealth and cunning, this invisible network has come to rule us all. Forty-one years after Shabbatai Zevi's death, in 1717, they would infiltrate Masonry guilds in England and establish Freemasonry... [Zevi's successor] Jacob Frank would have a great impact on the inner core of Freemasonry known as the Illuminati, formed in 1776. Freemasonry would become the hidden force behind events like the [American, French and Russian] revolutions, the creations of the U.N. & Israel, both World Wars (including the Holocaust!), and the assassinations of the Kennedy brothers who, together with their father, tried to thwart the efforts of the network on American soil. Sabbatean/Frankists, also referred to as the "Cult of the All-Seeing Eye" (look at your one dollar bill to begin to understand their influence in YOUR life) are political and religious chameleons. They are everywhere there is power. They are the good guys AND the bad guys. The World War Two era is a prime example. (24)

David Livingstone, author of Terrorism and the Illuminati: A Three Thousand Year History, says that all occult movements originate in the Kabbalah (which he dates to the 6th century B.C. Babylon), maintaining that most Illuminati bloodlines, including European royalty, are heretical Jews and crypto Jews (Jews who pretend they are from other religions). (26)

In his book, Livingstone details how the Kabbalist bankers, operating through their control of Saudi Arabia, the Bank of England and British/American Imperialism, conspired to break up the Ottoman Empire and keep the Middle East backward. He also meticulously explains how this shadow world government continues to use a variety of cults like Wahhabism (1700's) and Salafi (1900's), and Masonic secret societies like the Muslim Brotherhood (1930's) to divide Islam, to create fanatical fundamentalism and to foster terror in preparation for the coming "War of Civilizations." (26)

Bibliography

1. Scholem, Gershom. *The Messianic Idea in Judaism: And Other Essays on Jewish Spirituality.* (NY: Schocken, 1971)

2. Livingstone, David. *The Holiness of Sin: Freud, the Frankfurt School and the Kabbalah.* (9-19-2013)

3. Schindeldecker, John. *Turkish Alevis Today.* (Istanbul: Sakhulu Sultan Kulliyesi Vakfi: 1998)

4. Moosa, Matti. *Extremist Shiites.* (Syracuse University Press: 1988)

5. Reb Yakov Leib HaKohain, Director of Donmeh West

6. Juri, Lina, *Under the Sign of the Scorpion: The Rise and Fall of the Soviet Empire* (2002)

7. Baigent, Leigh and Lincoln. Holy Blood, Holy Grail: The Secret History of Christ & The Shocking Legacy of the Grail. (Dell Trade Paperbacks: 2004)

8. Chamish, Barry. *Shabtai Tzvi, Labor Zionism and the Holocaust.* (Modiin House: 2005)

9. Springmeier, Fritz. *The Illuminati Formula to Create an Undetectable Total Mind Control.* (CreateSpace: 2008)

10. Rabow, Jerry. *The Untold Life Stories of 50 Jewish Messiahs.* (Gefen: 2002)

11. Antelman, Rabbi Marvin. *To Eliminate the Opiate* (Volume 2) (The Zionist Book Club: 2002)

12. Miller, Edith Starr. *Occult Theocrasy.* Abbeville. (1933)

13. Makow, PHD, Henry. *Illuminati: The Cult That Hijacked the World* (Silas green: 2008)

14. Dilling, Elizabeth. *The Jewish Religion: Its Influence Today.* (1964)

15. Quigley, Carroll. *Tragedy and Hope: A History of the World in Our Time*. (GSG and Associates: 1966)

16. Makow, PhD, Henry. *The Root Problem: Illuminati Or Jews?* (2006)

17. Pike, Albert. *Morals and Dogma*. (1871)

18. Blavatsky, H.P. *The Secret Doctrine*. (1888)

19. Chamish, Barry. *The Deutsch Devils*. (2003)

20. Chamish, Barry. *Is This God's Israel?* (2010)

21. Herzl, Theodor. *The Complete Diaries of Theodor Herzl*. edited by Raphael Patai, Harry Zohn, (Herzla Press: 1960)

22. Morris, Benny. *Righteous Victims*. p. 21 (2001)

23. Bacque, James. *Crimes and Mercies*. (Vintage: 1997)

24. Shack, Clifford. *The Rothschilds, Winston Churchill and the Final Solution*. (2007)

25. Bjerknes, Christopher Jon. *The Jewish Genocide of Armenian Christians*. (2007, Enlarged Second Edition)

26. Livingstone, David. *Terrorism and the Illuminati: A Three-Thousand-Year History*. (2011)

27. Scholem,Gershom. *The Messianic Idea in Judaism and Other Essays on Jewish Spirituality*. New York: Schocken (1971)

28. Scholem, Gershom. *On the Kabbalah and Its Symbolism*. Translated: Ralph Manheim. New York: Schocken (1965)

29. Mullins, Eustace. *The Secrets of the Federal Reserve*. (1983)

30. Mullins, Eustace. *New World Order: Our Secret Rulers*. (1992)

31. Lazar, Bernard. *L'Anti-semitisme*. (1894)

32. Pike, Albert. *Morals and Dogma*, Third Degree, p. 104-105

33. Sutton, Anthony. *America's Secret Establishment: An Introduction to the Order of Skull & Bones*, P.6

34. Burns, Dr. Cath. *Masonic and Occult Symbols Illustrated*.

35. Gardiner, Philip. *Skull and Crossbones The Untold Tale of the Templar Shining Ones.* (2007)

36. Antelman, Rabbi Marvin S. *To Eliminate the Opiate (Volume 1).* (Zahavia: 1974)

37. Waterfield, Robin. *Why Socrates Died: Dispelling the Myths.* (W.W. Norton & Company: 2009)

38. Forces Occultes ("Occult Forces") Director: Jean Mamy, (March 10, 1943)

39. Gardiner, Philip. *Skull and Bones: Untold tale of the Templar Shining ones,* (2007)

40. Unterman, Alan. *An Anthology of Jewish Mysticism,* (2009)

41. Verdera, Nito. *The connection between Ibiza and Christopher Columbus's enigma.* (2000)

42. Loring Knowles, Christopher. *Another History of the Knights Templar,* (2011)

43. Taylor, A.J.P. *Sarajevo to Potsdam.* (Harcourt Brace Jovanovich: 1975)

44. Freedman, Benjamin. *A Jewish Defector Warns America: Benjamin Freedman Speaks.* (1961)

45. Schacht, Dr. Hjalmar. *The Magic of Money.* (Horace Greeley: 1967)

46. Schlottman, Konst. "Die sogenannte Inschrift von Parahyba"(ZDMG xxviii, (1874) pp. 481-487)

47. Grunberger, R. *The Twelve-Year Reich.* (Da Capo Press: 1976)

Images

Figure 1 - Sabbatai Zevi in 1665. Illustration from Brockhaus and Efron Jewish Encyclopedia (1906—1913)

Figure 2 - "Sabbatai Zevi enthroned", from Tikkun, Amsterdam, 1666.

Figure 3 - Jewish Kabbalist Holding a Sephiroth, Scan of an Illustration from "Portae Lucis"

Figure 4 - Helena Petrovna Blavatsky, 1889, London

Figure 5 – Right: Jacob Frank's skull, it was extracted from his grave in Offenbach when the old cemetery was razed in 1866, and is owned by Emil Pirazzi. The image is from Alexander Kraushar's book, Frank i frankiści polscy, 1726-1816 Vol. 2, as is the image to the left of Jacob Frank.

Figure 6 - Ewa (Awacza) Frank (1754-1816). Historical Monograph, Krakow 1895

Figure 7 - Adam Weishaupt (1748-1830)

Figure 8 - Scan of Albert Pike. Library of Congress, Washington, D.C.

Figure 9 – Skull & Bones sketch. Atlantean Gardens, Inc.

Figure 10 - Phoenician ship Carved on the face of a sarcophagus. 2nd century AD.

Figure 11 - A coin of Constantine (c.337) showing a depiction of his labarum spearing a serpent.

Figure 12 - modified scan of Faust's vision by Luis Ricardo Falero (1851–1896)

Figure 13 - Balfour Declaration as published in The Times 9 November 1917

Figure 14 - This is a poster for Forces Occultes. Written by Jean Marquès-Rivière. Produced by Robert Muzard. Directed by Jean Mamy. Distributed by Nova films. France. Release date: 10 March 1943.

Figure 15 - constructed from a 1938 newspaper clipping

Figure 16 - Altar of Burnt Offering. artist: anon

Figure 17 - Theodor Herzl. 1897

Made in the USA
Las Vegas, NV
26 December 2023

83518952R00046